THE CRAP
SECRET SANTA
GIFT BOOK

HEADLINE

Cataloguing in Publication Data is available from the British Library

Hardback ISBN 978 1 4722 4394 2

Designed by Beau Merchant at Toy Solder Creative

Illustrations on pages 10, 15, 18, 28 and 42 by Tom Noble

Printed and bound in the UK by Clays Ltd, Elcograf S.p.A.

Headline's policy is to use papers that are natural, renewable and recyclable
products and made from wood grown in sustainable forests. The logging and
manufacturing processes are expected to conform to the environmental
regulations of the country of origin.

HEADLINE PUBLISHING GROUP
An Hachette UK Company
Carmelite House
50 Victoria Embankment
London
EC4Y 0DZ

www.headline.co.uk
www.hachette.co.uk

Dedicated to George McGill
(inventor of the stapler)…

PICTURE CREDITS

…and Frumpty Smoothblender
(inventor of that little claw-thing
that helps remove them)

⚠ WARNING

ARE YOU THINKING OF LEAVING A BIT OF TINSEL
ON YOUR COMPUTER OR A NOVELTY ELF ON YOUR
DESK BEFORE YOU LEAVE FOR CHRISTMAS? THROW
THEM AWAY NOW UNLESS YOU WANT TO BE EVEN
MORE MISERABLE WHEN YOU COME BACK TO
WORK IN JANUARY WITH A TWO-WEEK HANGOVER,
SWEATING QUALITY STREET THROUGH YOUR KNEES
AND SILENTLY CRYING.

INTRODUCTION

Hello [Marketing Person / IT Guy / Boss]!

Season's greetings to you my wonderful colleague and friend.

Remember that conference / time we stood next to each other during the fire drill / time we stood next to each other on the bus pretending not to notice each other? Ah, heady days!

I do hope you enjoy this well-thought-through Secret Santa present. You know those lazy, tossed-off efforts that you just buy because you think it might possibly raise a smile for about half an hour? Well, it's not as good as one of those, obviously, but I bet you'll be using it to steady a table in the pub a bit later on.

Either that, or you could attempt to eat it whole on January 2nd and have a legitimate excuse to throw a sickie. It's win-win.

Yours,
Secret Santa

This is the loneliest mince pie in the world.
He died at the age of 47.
Milk bottles piled up outside the front door.
The TV left on.
Junk mail backed up in the hall.
Some say he died of a broken heart.

Everyone bangs on about dogs this time of year.
Please remember mince pies.

OFFICE CHRISTMAS PARTY TIPS

It's December 8th and it's the Christmas party. 'I'll just stay for a couple,' you say with spritely optimism. The next thing you know you're wailing along to 'The Fairytale of New York' and thinking that Kevin in accounts looks rather attractive in that snazzy cardigan. Keep these tips in mind if you want to survive…

1. Eat everything in sight. Crisps, Maltesers, belly-button fluff – whatever. Don't be that person drinking gin out of a shoe and crying bitter tears as someone pours you into a taxi half an hour after you've got there.

2. Call it quits early. Ideally, before the party's actually started. Nothing good has ever happened after 9pm at the Office Christmas Party. This is the time when Brian from Digital Marketing starts putting his big sausage fingers on people's knees. Get out of there!

3. Prepare some conversation topics. There's a good chance you're going to be stuck on a table in the pub with a bunch of people you are practised at avoiding eye contact with. This will be awkward. But less so if you've got some snappy one-liners ready. Try these on for size:

'Who was the last person *you* killed?'

'What's the point in anything?' (This should be whispered to whoever's closest.)

'Which one of us do you think most looks like they should be on a "register"?'

"He who does not put the milk back in the fridge in the communal kitchen is definitely a massive p***k."

Ancient Proverb

STUFF I COULD HAVE BOUGHT YOU INSTEAD OF THIS BOOK (PART 1)

A Cup of Pretentious Coffee

RRP: £3.50

This top of the range SputnikShitStorm 5000 Coffee Machine is capable of brewing several gallons per minute of pumpkin-spiced Alpacino whizzbinder-bean artisanally-sourced coffee.

0-60 in 4.7 seconds

Coffee best served in a tiny little glass without a handle

Coffee best consumed sitting on an uncomfortable wooden crate

Music to listen to whilst you drink: Bolivian Jazz

TWENTY CHRISTMAS NUMBER ONES YOU MAY HAVE FORGOTTEN

1. *I Believe That Children Aren't The Future* – Sizzle Jenkins & The Wangs

2. *I Am Not Afraid Of You* – Toby Puy-Lentil

3. *Tit For Tat* – Stephanie Unlikely

4. *It's Christmas, You Pathetic Worm* – Dilly Shingles

5. *You Can't Even Call It Christmas These Days, Can You?* – The Middle Englanders

6. *Yes, You Can* – The Rest of the Country

7. *Last Christmas I Gave You My Priceless Collection of Porcelain Frogs* – Tricky Dicky & The Screaming

8. *Lists Are Hard, Especially At Christmas* – The Number Eights

9. *The Winner's Song* – Nathan Radcliffe, X Factor Winner 2007*

10. *What Time Is It Acceptable To Start Drinking, Do You Reckon?* – Bunty McMump

11. *Hide The Sausage* – Billy Wigwam & The Trots

12. *What Was That Bloke In Again, The One Playing Scrooge?* – Ethel & The Grandmas

13. *Christmas Is Bleak, When The Telly's So Sh*t* – Jimmy Stickleback & The Cracks

14. *What Do You Mean, 'Myrrh'?* – Jeezy Big Beard's Crazy Crew

15. *You Invited Me Over For Christmas Day And Left Me With The Coffee Creams You Utter Bastard* – Timothy Ball-Boy

16. *I've Definitely Left The Price Tag On That* – Boon Wallace and the Horny Caterpillars

17. *Last Christmas I Gave You The Impression That I Loved You, But I've Since Spent Boxing Day With Your Creepy Uncle And Now I Want To Hide And Cry* – Helen Central-Reservation

18. *Gravy, Gravy Everywhere, I Shouldn't Have Had That Last Gin* – Jippety Trollop & The Outrageous Trombones

19. *The Regular Version Of That Song That's Been Covered In Godawfully Mawkish Style By Some Popstar Or Other To Help A Supermarket Sell Crisps* – The Swindon Swingers

20. *Why Would You Bother Getting Your Dog A Present? Look, It Cares More About The Wrapping Paper Anyway For God's Sake, So Grow Up* – Diddly Fluffwagon

*Made up, obviously, but you had to think about it didn't you?

Dear Santa...

...featuring Morrissey

Dear Santa,

I hope you're well.

I'd like to say it's been a good year, but, alas, fate has conspired against me once more. Just this morning I went to get some tofu from the fridge and slipped on some errant baked beans that had been spilled on the lino. By whom, it's impossible to say. Must I suffer such injustice on a daily basis?

Anyhoo, here's a list of some trivial possessions it would be marvellous to receive this Christmas. Though I'm not expecting much. Obviously.

My Christmas List

Hair wax. My quiff is all.
New shirts. Really must stop hurling them at the 45-year-old men who love me so.
The gift of eternal life.
Stamps.
Light bulbs. That light's gonna go out one day...

I'm sure there's more, but, alas, I must take to the stage once again.

Please, Please, Please let me get what I want. (That joke isn't funny any more, is it?)

Your pal,
Morrissey

GAMES TO PLAY DURING MEETINGS

'Shall I set up a pre-pre-meeting for the pre-meeting
for the meeting?'

'No, Steve. Why don't you go and sit in the corner
and think about what you've done?'

1. Every time someone uses the phrase 'Key Performance Indicators', imagine them covered in marmalade, stumbling blindly towards some angry, horny wasps.

2. Slip in a made-up word and see if people notice. Examples could include:

- Blibberation
- Spandle
- Flimp
- Shizbit
- Janitorially
- Bundlecump

3. Make the following fake phonecall:

'Hi. I can't really talk now. Right. Well how many snakes? Jesus, that's twice as many as last week. Well, release the monkeys and let's hope for the best.' **hang up** 'Sorry everyone, where were we?'

4. Prime a colleague that whenever you start to speak they should 'accidentally' interrupt you. You should then continue the following loop for the entirety of the meeting:

'Sorry, go on.'
'No, you go first.'
'Sorry, go on.'
'No, you go first.'
'Sorry, go on.'
'No, you go first.'
'Sorry, go on.'

FUN FACT!

Cygnophobia or *kiknophobia* is the fear of swans.

Look at this guy. Looks innocent enough, doesn't he (or she. Haven't checked)? In fact, he (or she) has a large collection of machetes and is hiding under your bed right now.

STUFF I COULD HAVE BOUGHT YOU INSTEAD OF THIS BOOK (PART 2)

Darius Off Of *Pop Idol's* Goatee Beard

RRP: £4.99

Many people think that Darius's incredible singing voice and
all-round talent were due to an innate natural ability or
years of hard work and training. In fact, it was the perfectly
manicured beard that adorned his beautiful face that helped him
perform so exquisitely in talent competitions in the early 2000s.
Now a bona fide West End star, it is time for this gathering of
incredible hairs to find a new owner – to help them reach for
the goddamn stars. But yeah, I got you this book instead. Sorry
about that.

SO IT COULD HAVE BROKEN YOU
INSTEAD OF THE BOOK INTO

OFFICE CHRISTMAS PARTY TIPS (CONTINUED)

SITTING WITH THE BOSS

So you've been sat opposite The Boss at the office party. You'd seen the table plan earlier but even though you tried to bribe Maureen on the Party Planning Committee™ with a half-eaten bag of Monster Munch she wouldn't budge.
Here's some tips on how to survive...

1. PRETEND YOU'VE GONE TEMPORARILY BLIND AND DEAF

It's a risky strategy, sure, but it might just work. It's key that you announce the blindness/deafness thing as soon as you've all sat down, and follow it up by saying 'I'm fine, I'm sure it's jut temporary' with your eyes fixed on a spot on the wall. Don't panic. Just wait for the starters to arrive and then revel in your deceit as you ladle lukewarm tomato soup into your lying face.

2. FAKE A SEIZURE

Obviously not one so big that you won't be able to down nine shots of tequila and kick someone in the face dancing to 'Driving Home For Christmas' about an hour later, but enough that you'll be carried off somewhere and given medical attention until pudding arrives.

3. HIDE

Once everyone's downed the luke-warm glass of champagne-style-fizzy-grape-water that the budget's stretched to, use the opportunity to sneak away and hide in the toilets where you will have hidden several Cornettos in the bathroom like a confectionery inspired Godfather. Here you shall live like a king, scoffing ice-cream and imagining The Boss questioning the person sat next to your empty chair about turnover and action points.

Dear Santa...

...featuring Nigel Farage

Dear Santa,

How are you old boy?

I love Christmas. I was actually there when it was invented in Guildford in 1978.

What I'd really love as a present is to go back to the good old days, where people had proper names like 'Ian' and 'Jane', and everyone dressed in Union Jack-themed clothes and ate Shepherd's Pie for breakfast. Sadly, that's not allowed now because of Brussels and their red tape. I know that sounds like a lie, but when have I ever lied to anyone, ever?

So here's my list, Santa old chap. As a jolly, red-faced man who appears for one day a year to bring joy to everyone in the land, you are a man after my own heart. So don't let me down.

My Christmas List

A bottle of good old fashioned English sauvignon blanc.

Keys to the town of Melton Mowbray.

A massive hunting horn for making fun noises with.

Sausage and Chips.

Loads of money that I will definitely spend on the thing I'll tell you I'm going to spend it on.

Right, I'm off for a well-earned lie down, a lovely big mug of Bovril and a cigar. Here's hoping I don't accidentally pour burning hot liquid all over my face and set fire to myself!

Your friend,
Nigel

LUNCH RECIPE

Here is a cost-effective yet delicious salad recipe to impress your pals at work!

INGREDIENTS

2 tbsp olive oil
1 tbsp cumin seeds
500g carrots
1 tbsp honey
1 red onion, finely sliced
½ Lemon
handful coriander
50g iceberg lettuce
75g feta cheese, crumbled

METHOD

1. Chop the carrots into batons and place in a large bowl, along with the red onion, olive oil, and cumin seeds. Mix well.

2. Roughly chop the lettuce and add to the bowl along with the juiced lemon, coriander and crumbled feta.

3. Throw this all in the bin, safe in the knowledge that you'll never actually make this salad because you'll be too hungover and you've realised you've only got twenty-five minutes to make your child's *Harry Potter* costume for World Book Day and all that's in the house is some Twiglets and half a sheet of a greaseproof paper.

TEN NICKNAMES TO CHOOSE WHEN YOU'VE STARTED A NEW JOB

There's a certain freedom that comes with starting a new job. You can reinvent yourself, just like when you went to uni and started wearing that hat that you thought made you look sexy and debonair but actually made you instantly repellent to women the moment you stepped into the lecture theatre and which you only realised three years too late and . . . sorry, you get the point.

Anyway, here are some cool nicknames you can try and pretend are yours when you start at a new job.

'Yeah, my name's James, but everyone calls me...'

1. Slasher
2. The Money
3. Flash
4. Gorgeous
5. The Fixer
6. Stinkazoid
7. Soggy
8. Armitage Shanks
9. Stephen Hendry
10. Jesus Christ Superstar

STUFF I COULD HAVE BOUGHT YOU INSTEAD OF THIS BOOK (PART 3)

Festival Survival Kit

RRP: £1.99

Includes:
1 x scissors

Use this incredible, mono-action mono-tool to systematically cut up every festival ticket you've bought for next year, so that instead of standing in the pouring rain in a poncho made from limp fennel trying to pour as much cider into your face as possible to drown out the sound of Bono singing, you're sitting at home in the living room in a paddling pool full of camembert watching it on the six new TVs you've spent the money on instead.

"Remember, it is a wise man
who doesn't send attachments
over 5mb but instead, like, uses
WeTransfer or whatever."

Ancient Proverb

TWELVE THINGS TO MAKE CONVERSATION ABOUT IN THE LIFT

Those fourteen seconds of lift chat can be awkward, sometimes to the extent that you'd rather suddenly plunge forty feet to your death than carry on. Here are some suggestions for topics you can bring up instead of just saying, 'This week seems to have gone on forever!'

1. Dungarees on Dogs
2. The Films of Adam Sandler
3. The GDP of Tonga
4. The Existential Angst of Wanting to Push People Into Traffic For No Reason
5. Swans*
6. Death
7. Inevitable, Inevitable Death
8. The Shirts of Noel Edmonds
9. French Horns
10. Regret
11. Worst Ever Ear Infection
12. Least Favourite Member of The Corrs

*Honestly, I can't quite explain just how much of a dangerous bastard that thing is. I saw it deck a heron once just for looking at it funny.

Dear Santa...

...featuring Bono Vox

Dearest St Nick,

As you know I never ask for much. In fact, asking for anything at all has got me all a quiver as I'm so used to giving things away (for free, to your iPhone, even if you don't want them).

What I'm after is a favour really. The thing is, I need The Edge gone. Taken out. Kaput. You know what I mean?

The last few months he's become unbearable. One minute he's right-as-rain and the next he explodes like the riff on 'In the Name of Love.'

Just last week he smashed up the kitchen at U2 HQ because someone had used the last of the almond butter. (He actually broke my LiveAid mug whilst on his rampage so could you maybe throw one of those in?)

Me and the other two have had enough so if you could maybe arrange some kinda horrible accident that would be grand.

All the best,
Bono

THE EXTERNAL MODERATOR:
A CASE STUDY

This is Brett. He's thirty-nine. He lives in a house with his wife Steph and his children Arthur and Tomato. He rides a Brompton. He has been to America. He is going to make you stand on increasingly small bits of newspaper and climb up a rope. He is being paid several million pounds an hour in the hope that forcing you to build a raft out of discarded kebab boxes will make you better at being an Air Traffic Controller.

"He who walks around the office in socks is not to be trusted."

Ancient Proverb

STUFF I COULD HAVE BOUGHT YOU
INSTEAD OF THIS BOOK (PART 4)

Seven Bees
RRP: £4.90

Includes: Well . . . seven bees.

Bees are all the rage. And by that I mean they are angry little
bastards. However, think of the sweet, sweet honey they
make. You would have been the envy of all your friends if
you'd received them instead of this book. The one constraint
is budget. A fiver gets you seven, possibly six if one's a bit
of a bloater. Also, this doesn't include the beekeeping suit or
the hive or anything, so keeping the little guys safe and sound
would be tricky. In fact, thinking about it, it would actually
be a nightmare. Good thing I got you this book then, right?!
RIGHT?!

FUN FACT!

You thought that last swan was bad. This one, honestly, and I'm not just saying this, is one of the most dangerous things in the entire world. You know that cliché about them being able to break someone's arm? Well I once saw this guy snap a boxer's neck just by coughing. Press covered it up of course. I'm just saying, don't trust him. OK?

GAMES TO PLAY DURING MEETINGS (PART 2)

1. Start the meeting by looking at everyone in turn and saying: 'One of you in this room shall one day betray me'. Then carry on as normal and make no further reference to it.

2. Strategically Sellotape snacks to the bottom of your chair. See how many biscuits you can eat before someone asks you where you're getting them from.

3. See how many times you can mention the former Aston Villa striker turned *Homes Under the Hammer* presenter Dion Dublin.

4. Inform those present that you suffer from Narcolopsey. 'For those of you who don't know, that means I will often fall asleep spontaneously, even halfway through a …' [Pretend to fall asleep]

5. When someone puts their mobile phone on the table, pick it up and examine it with childlike wonder, as if it's the most magical thing you've ever seen. Then become tearful and start screaming, 'Witch! WITTTTCH!'

MORNING SNACK RECIPE

Another delicious treat!

INGREDIENTS
3 eggs
250ml semi-skimmed milk
110 vegetable oil
200g golden caster sugar
400g self-raising flour
80g chocolate chips
1 tsp salt

METHOD

1. Pre-Heat the oven to 200C. Line a muffin tray with paper muffin cases. Beat the eggs for one-two minutes. Add oil and milk and beat until combined. Add the sugar and whisk, then sift in flour and salt. Mix in the chocolate chips.

2. Fill muffin cases and bake for 25 minutes, until risen. Transfer to wire rack and leave to cool.

3. Carefully strap the muffins over your ears before you go to bed. Not only will you sleep through your alarm you will then have a delicious, delicious morning snack to eat in bed as you practise your best 'sorry boss, can't come in today' voice. Textbook.

TWELVE THINGS TO MAKE CONVERSATION ABOUT IN THE LIFT (PART 2)

So you've exhausted 1-12, and now you've got six floors to go. Maybe there was an Adam Sandler movie you forgot to talk about (the guy's got an extraordinary oeuvre, of course), or maybe you never had an ear infection. Either way, you need some new topics in case someone asks you about what you've got coming up at the weekend and all you can think of is drinking whisky in the shed and crying.

13. What it Actually is That Meatloaf Won't Do For Love

14. Best Way to Stop a Swan Attack

15. Wild, Speculative Guesses on Office Affairs

16. Who Would Win in a Fist Fight Between Donald Trump and Art Attack Presenter Neil Buchanan

17. Most Inappropriate Place to Play Hopskotch

18. Who You Would Eat First in the Event of Getting Trapped in This Lift

19. Would You Wait Till They Were Actually Dead?

20. Do Any of Us Really Die?

21. What if We're Reincarnated As, Say, a Pebble?

22. I Once Saw a Pebble That Looked Like Nicolas Lyndhurst

23. Have You Ever Seen a Pebble or Other 'Clast' of Rock That Resembled a Beloved English Actor?

24. Spiders

> **"It's fine to bring your new child into work. But do not humorously refer to them as your new assistant."**
>
> **Ancient Proverb**

A READY-MADE POST-IT NOTE TO LEAVE IN THE FRIDGE

Dear colleague,

I regret to inform you I have stolen and eaten your leftover edamame beans / chick-pea goulash / pheasant and cheddar wrap / weird-looking soup etc.

Please be assured that the only reason I decided to steal and then eat the above was because your passive-aggressive note last week imploring people not to steal and eat the above was a) annoying and b) written in comic sans.

Kind regards,
The Person Eating Your Food Right Now

Dear Santa...

...featuring Kanye West

42

Dear Santa,

My name is Kanye Omari West. I am 39 years old. I like dancing under really low lights, trainers and making music with my friends. It's really fun!

For Christmas I would really REALLY love to get the Transformers Rescue Bots Electronic Fire Station Prime Playset. I have been really good this year.

If I can't get that, I would like:

- A Sodastream
- Fifty clothes pegs (ALL red plastic, not wooden)
- Tremors 2 on DVD
- Some colouring pencils
- Sea Monkeys
- HMV vouchers

I hope all that is OK, Santa? I can't WAIT for Christmas to come now! SOOOO excited!

Take it Yeezy,
Kanye

TEN PRESENTS YOU WILL GET THIS CHRISTMAS THAT YOU DON'T REALLY WANT
(INCLUDING THIS BOOK)

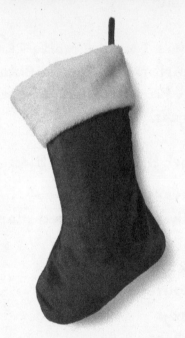

'It's a ten-thousand-piece Peter Andre puzzle! Remember? You said you liked him once in 1996. What's that? Oh yeah I got it from the car boot. No, not a car boot sale, I just found it in the car boot. Must have been there for ages, thinking about it. Why are you crying?'

1. A deodorant / shower gel combo pack from your Nan from a brand called 'Smooth Guy'.

2. An autobiography of an 80s footballer you've never heard of who played for England seven times and once had an altercation with an off duty policeman in a service station near Uttoxeter.

3. A massive bag of chocolate money that you will rip open desperately and painfully with your fingers because the scissors are approximately three feet away.

4. Socks with individual days of the week on them that you will initially stick to diligently before throwing caution to the wind and wearing Thursday on Monday. This will be the most rebellious act of your life until Wednesday on Friday.

5. A calendar with dogs wearing different sorts of hats that you'll never hang up.

6. A self-help book that casually alludes to a perceived weakness that you weren't actually aware of, e.g. '7 Ways To Stop Being So Terrible At Everything You Attempt.'

7. A candle the size of your own head called something pretentious like Hummingbird Whisper.

8. This book.

9. This book again. (My word you've got lazy colleagues / relatives / friends. Actually, lazy friends is unfair. You haven't got any friends, have you?)

10. 1,000 liqueur chocolates. Because everyone likes rum and custard combined in a mouth-sized lump.

Remember that lonely mince pie from the start?
Turns out it was all a vicious rumour.
He's alive and well, living in Cheltenham with a wife
and two kids.
He runs a successful second-hand car dealership and
enjoys holidays in the south of France.

Sorry for any distress this may have caused.

A BUNCH OF EXCUSES TO GET OFF WORK THE DAY AFTER THE CHRISTMAS PARTY

Oh God. It's 8:36 in the morning. You've woken up, for reasons that are unclear, in the bath. You have used a Pot Noodle as a pillow. Your knees hurt. You crawl to find your phone. You have 3% battery and the last message is from 'John – Sales' and reads: 'No need to apologise. It was just a misunderstanding. Hope you get back OK!' It's clear you won't be going in to work today, but you need a decent excuse. Take a deep breath and prepare to call your boss with one of the following fool-proof reasons why you won't be making it in today...

1. I bumped into Chris Akabusi and joined in the search for his missing pet stick insect.

2. I was admitted to A&E with an unprecedented case of severe Ice-Cream Headache.

3. Wasps.

4. The temporary blindness came back.

5. Someone posted an extraordinary amount of ham through my letter box.

6. I got mugged by six swans working as a team.

7. What I initially thought was a slice of toast turned out to be 1971 Ford Anglia.

8. Don't you see? I've been dead for years! I've been haunting your every waking moment! But not today. I've got the runs. Big time.

9. Did I not say? I am a member of a religion which you are fairly sure is fictitious but are too scared to challenge me on and it is our special holy day that involves watching re-runs of *Diagnosis: Murder* and eating crisps.

10. I've thought long and hard, but I've come to the conclusion that this job is just a complete and utter waste of f*****g time.

CRACKER JOKES
THAT DIDN'T MAKE THE CUT

After going into administration last year, Christmas cracker makers Stroodle Parker & Son had their offices raided by the bailiffs. At the bottom of a pile of papers there was a folder marked "Rejected Cracker Jokes – Please Burn".

Here's what was inside...

What happened to the woman who ironed the curtains?

She fell out of the window

How many footballers does it take to change a lightbulb?

Well it depends on the footballer in question. Frank Lampard seems a fairly intelligent chap so maybe just one of him whereas someone like Wayne Rooney would struggle so maybe 5 or even 6 of him! LOL!

Why did the fisherman have a magnifying glass?

He was FISHING!

Knock-Knock.

Who's there?

You just said it!

What?

Doctor Who.

Please go away.

Why does Tom Cruise drive at 30mph?

Because he's CRUUUUISING!

"He who tells a story to colleagues once should remember who he's told so as not to repeat it for the 25th time over lunch."

Ancient Proverb

FUN FACT!

For the last few days I've had the feeling I'm being followed. At first I put it down to being paranoid, but I've seen him. He's everywhere I go. Those dark vacant eyes and that... Oh no. Please. Not like this. It was never meant to end like this...

...I warned you!

No!! Please!!

Listen, let's just talk
about th_##AAh++@!!!AAHH_!!